# THINKING ABOUT
# EDUCATION

World Development General Editor: John P. Reardon
Departmental Secretary of the Church and Society Department
of the United Reformed Church

# THINKING ABOUT EDUCATION

## KRISTER OTTOSSON

*Adviser in Lay Training on the Durham Diocesan
Board of Education*

LUTTERWORTH EDUCATIONAL
GUILDFORD AND LONDON

First published 1978

For Katherine

**ISBN 0 7188 2301 X**

Printed in Great Britain by
Fletcher & Son Ltd, Norwich

# CONTENTS

# LIST OF ILLUSTRATIONS

The author and publishers wish to express their gratitude to the United Society for the Propagation of the Gospel for permission to reproduce illustrations nos. 1, 2, 3 (with the Methodist Missionary Society), 7, 8, 10 and 11; and Claudius—Institut d'Action Culturelle, Geneva for nos. 4, 5, 6, 9, 12, 13, 14 and 15.

# EDITOR'S INTRODUCTION

Ever since space-ships began to send back pictures of the earth we have realized the truth of the cliché that we all live in one world. Yet we have come increasingly to realize also that it is a world of deep divisions, none more tragic than that between the rich and the poor. Throughout history the conflicts within nations between the rich and the poor, the powerful and the weak, have caused political upheavals, social revolutions and much suffering and misery. Today those same conflicts, still present within nations, threaten the relationships between nations. Some suggest that the greatest single threat to world peace is the fact that two-thirds of the world's population live in conditions of poverty and deprivation.

The First Development Decade of the United Nations, in the 1960s, suggested that the problem of development for the poorer nations could largely be overcome by greatly increased aid from the rich to the poor, combined with economic growth in the developing countries. The conventional approach to development was through economics. Throughout those years the poorer nations increased their agricultural and industrial output, but in spite of overseas aid, largely in fact in the form of loans which they are still repaying, the gap between them and the rich nations widened. We no longer believe that the problems of the poor can simply be solved by the generosity of the rich.

The Second Development Decade of the 1970s, while still stressing the economic basis for development, has forced us to realize that there will be no real breakthroughs until we see world development as a process in which the rich and poor nations begin to recognize their interdependency and begin to see development in human and not just economic terms. More and more we are coming to see that the process of world development involves all the people of the earth.

Through a series of Special Sessions and international conferences, the United Nations has focused on many of the outstanding problems and challenges confronting the presently divided world community. Thinking particularly of the majority of the poorer countries, the UN Special Sessions of 1974 and 1975 addressed themselves to the acute problems, following the oil crisis and the huge increases in the price of oil, and issued a call for a new international economic order which would lead to a more just distribution of the world's resources, and would attempt to harmonize the interests of the rich and poor countries by speeding up the economic and social progress of the latter. Conferences like the World Population Conference of 1974, the World Food Conference of 1974, and the World Employment Conference of 1976 have given opportunity for governments to see the many dimensions of development and have underlined the fact that most of the development problems have to be solved by the world, rather than simply by the third world, community.

This series attempts to show how many-sided world development is. Each book deals with one aspect and explores the complexity of development as a whole, showing just how extensive are its dimensions. The series also attempts to show how the problem of development not only concerns what happens in countries far away, but has important links with and implications for our own lives.

Most of the world's great religions emphasize man's stewardship of the earth's resources, grapple with problems of evil and suffering, and speak about peace and human brotherhood. It is, therefore, not surprising that religious education teachers have found themselves face to face with the problems of world development touching so many of the great religious themes. In their search for meaning in life pupils must face the realities of the world as it is, and must begin to see their own lives in relation to the puzzling and daunting conditions in which so many of their contemporaries throughout the world are growing up. We hope that these books will provide teachers of many subjects with a common basis and starting-point for co-operation in helping pupils to discover some links between history, geography, economics, culture, politics, sociology and religious studies.

*John Reardon*

# SUGGESTIONS FOR FURTHER READING

WCC *Study Encounter:*
    vol. X, no. 2, 1974: Karl Ernst Nipkow, 'Education for Liberation and Community'.
    vol. VIII, no. 2, 1972: William B. Kennedy, 'Encuentros: A New Ecumenical
      Learning Experience'.
    vol. IX, no. 1, 1973: Paulo Freire, 'Education, Liberation and the Church'.
UNESCO: *Learning to Be.*
WCC (Theological Education Fund): *Learning in Context.*
CEM *Learning for Living:* 'Is School Dead?' January 1974.

Paulo Freire, *Education for Critical Consciousness* (Sheed & Ward).
Paulo Freire, *Pedagogy of the Oppressed* (Sheed & Ward).
E. F. Schumacher, *Small Is Beautiful* (Abacus).
John Sutcliffe, *Learning Community* (Denholm House Press).
Brian Wren, *Education for Justice* (SCM Press).

# 1

## EXPERIMENTS AND NEW IDEAS

### INDIA

**The Background**

The first universities in the world were those of the Brahmins in India. Their aim was to provide an education which was based on philosophy and religion while at the same time stressing the study of mathematics, history, astronomy and the laws of economics. Therefore, because of India's great educational tradition, the Christian missionaries to that continent regarded it as important that they set up large numbers of schools and colleges.

At the Third Annual Conference of Christian Schools in India in May 1975, one speaker said:

> The Christian community of India has established a network of educational institutions which is unmatched in the world in its extent, variety and quality. The 16 million strong Christian community is today responsible for more than 10,000 elementary schools, 2,000 high schools, 174 colleges, 273 technical schools and a couple of dozen institutions for the handicapped. These institutions cater for the needs of $4\frac{1}{2}$ million Indian children of whom half are not Christians.

The government, also, has regarded education as being of prime importance: several states spend up to 55% of their annual budget on education.

Yet, in spite of this national emphasis on education, in 1975 it was claimed that 60% of the population was illiterate and a larger proportion still was uneducated: mass education had not 'caught on'. The majority of Indian people appeared to regard formal education as irrelevant to their lives. Only one-third of children between the ages of 11 and 14 were enrolled in schools.

1. Sangli New English School at Kolharpur in western India.

## The Problem

Lord Macaulay said that the aim of British education in India in the nineteenth century was to produce 'a class of persons, Indian in blood and colour, but English in tastes, opinions, in morals and intellect'.

John Henry Newman, in a famous essay entitled *The Idea of a University*, wrote:

> Liberal Education does not make the Christian, but the gentleman. It is well to be a gentleman; it is well to have a cultivated intellect, a delicate taste. A habit of mind is formed, a candid, equitable, dispassionate mind, a noble and courteous bearing. These are the concomitants of a larger knowledge, they are the objects of a University.

Clearly such a philosophy of education is largely irrelevant to a predominantly rural nation living at a low level of subsistence, and where children are regarded by their parents as investments for the future — the more hands there are in the family to help till the soil the better they can withstand the ravages of poverty. Increasingly, therefore, the wisdom of the

14

2. Making rugs at the Sisal Handicrafts Factory at Ahmadnagar in western India.

great Indian thinkers like Gandhi and Tagore has come to be recognized by educationalists, particularly their insistence that an education unrelated to the social and economic environment in which people live alienates the student from his community and in the end does more harm than good both to the student himself and to the community.

## Three Experiments

There are a number of educational experiments being tried in various parts of India by a variety of organizations, including the government and the churches. The most significant of them are attempting to combine the more important elements of schooling (teaching people to read and write) with practical work relevant to their lives (like growing crops and repairing farm tools).

*Intensive Educational District Development Projects*
These projects are being tried in four states: Punjab, Bihar, Maharashtra and Mysore. About $9\frac{1}{2}$ million people are involved. The aim is to provide a relevant education for all the people in a community between the ages of 3 and 45. They are directed towards everybody — those previously in some sector of education, those who have dropped out of education, whether as children or adults, and those with no education at all. They include full-time as well as part-time courses at various centres, and radio broadcasts. Each project is tailor-made to meet the needs of a particular district. The idea is to help the members of each community become aware of their needs, and then help them learn together how to meet those needs. Thus adults and children might find themselves in the same class or group learning about crop rotation.

An important element of the projects is flexibility: for instance, in order that small children might help their families in the fields, the school day has in some cases been reduced. The effect is that elementary schools can run on a two-shift basis, enabling the same number of teachers to teach more children, and enabling other children from the same family to attend different school shifts.

*The Young Farmers' Institute in Lucknow*
Literacy House in Lucknow is a large house with many acres of grounds. One of its aims is to banish illiteracy. But its supporters believe that the most effective way in which to teach people to read, write and count is by getting them to talk and learn more about the things that matter most to them — their crops, their homes, their families, and their farming equipment. Literacy House therefore uses its grounds to demonstrate new agricultural methods and strains of crops. While much of the work of the staff is done at the House itself, a great deal of it involves work in the surrounding villages where practical help is given to farmers, on the understanding that the aim is always to help them make better use of their land. While the farmers experiment with new methods, they learn about crop yields, nutritional values, family hygiene, technology and machines. The term used to describe this kind of education is 'functional literacy' — when a person is functionally literate he is literate in the things which relate to his everyday existence.

*Theological Education*
At Arasaradi in South India the Tamilnadu Theological Seminary trains young men for the priesthood. The particular theological training it provides is unique. Whereas most theological colleges in various parts of

3. Children in a slum area (*favela*) in São Paulo, Brazil.

the world emphasize a study of the creeds, church history, religious worship and the Bible, at Arasaradi prospective priests learn what the Christian faith is all about through practical involvement in the world.

The seminary sees itself as part of the local community identifying with and sharing its problems. It runs a 'fair-price' shop for people in the local neighbourhood, and a centre for children from a nearby slum area of the town. It has developed a debt-relief programme for villagers who were previously paying as much as 300% interest on loans. The leaders of 27 slum communities have received training in mass education in order to enable them to organize the people to campaign for better conditions.

In this way the students at the seminary find themselves deeply involved in political conflict. They believe that it is precisely through such involvement with the sufferings of ordinary men and women who are their fellow human beings that they learn what Christians ought to mean when they speak of caring for the poor and needy: it is a caring which involves identification with their suffering, and action to bring about a more just society.

17

# LATIN AMERICA

## Three Points of View

A speaker from Argentina said at the World Council of Churches Consultation on Education in 1970 at Bergen, Holland: 'What's the good of talking about instilling a sense of beauty when the only beautiful things you can see as you look around on the hunger and exploitation of the third world are luxury hotels for foreign tourists?'

In a part of the city of Lima, in Peru, where the poor people live, two women were talking. Both of them had large families, and as well as caring for their children, they also had to care for elderly relatives. Their husbands worked long hours for low wages. The apartments in which they lived each had three small rooms. The two families had to share a communal kitchen with two other families. One of the women, who belonged to a neighbourhood association, said that the other people in the area had to be stirred up to protest against their living conditions. The friend said that this was not a Christian thing to do, so the first woman said:

'Don't you think that Jesus Christ came into the world to make it more like the place that God wanted it to be?'

'Yes,' said the other.

'And don't you think that Jesus Christ wanted his followers to help him make that better world?'

'Yes.'

'Then you can't be a Christian and let things remain as they are.'

A speaker from Brazil at the Bergen Consultation mentioned above argued that Latin American nations needed social changes which would alter the fundamental structures of society: these changes were so far-reaching that it would not be possible to bring them about without violence and conflict. Education, he argued, must be concerned with preparing people for that conflict. His name was Claudius Ceccon, some of whose cartoons are included in this book.

## The Hidden Consequences of Education

Look at the cartoon. What is it trying to say?

Claudius drew this cartoon because it encapsulated for him the way in which many thoughtful people in the Latin American countries felt about their dependence on the United States of America, and how education

4. Education with a purpose?

served only to increase his nation's dependence on America. And if a particular education served to make people more dependent rather than more free, then there was something wrong with that education.

On April 27, 1971, Dr. Salvador Allende, then President of Chile, addressed the Assembly of the Economic Commission of Latin America. He said:

> Every day more and more of us reject the existing system, and with reason. We must persist in raising those horrendous statistics so often repeated by you in a voice of warning, so often repeated by us in a voice of suffering, and so often unheard by so many. More than 30% of our population is illiterate: 80 million people. 11% of the total labour force is unemployed: 9 million individuals. 28% of the labourers underemployed: 75 million people who contribute only minimally to the development of the region. Each person consumes an average of 1,550 calories daily as against over 3,000 in the developed countries: 65 grams of protein a day (when he eats) compared to more than 100 grams in the countries of Europe. Here is the malnutrition, chronic hunger, the wasting away and the irreparable brain damage. Year after year foreign investors have obtained benefits far greater than the amounts invested. Since 1962 the profits removed from Latin America exceed the investments by more than a billion dollars. *Since the middle of the decade of the sixties our payments for debt-servicing are higher than the new loans made.*

## The Task

Many Christians in Latin America believe that President Allende's protest against the unjust world economic structures echoed some of the most strident passages in the Bible in which those who tolerated or participated in injustice were condemned and warned that the time had come for things to change. (See the Book of Amos, Psalm 12, and James 5.)

Many Christians also believe it is through education that a change can be made in the basic attitudes of people — a change of attitudes which must come before there can be any worthwhile changes in the economic and social structures of society. Christian educationalists in Latin America feel that the high illiteracy rate is partly due to the apathy in a large proportion of the population — an apathy brought about by powerful social and economic structures which have made ordinary people feel helpless. Because they feel themselves born into a condition that they are powerless to change, their whole lives become apathetic, and they can't see the point of education.

Therefore, if people are to be helped to become literate, the literacy education they receive has to relate to the feelings that they have about the social conditions in which they find themselves.

20

5. Who needs education?

One of the most successful Christian educationalists in Latin America in recent years has been Paulo Freire. A more detailed account of his work is given in a later chapter (see page 66). Here it is sufficient to indicate briefly the principles on which he has worked, principles which his successors have developed extensively all over the continent, as well as in other parts of the world.

The main aim is to help adults become literate. A group of people would be brought together into what was called a 'cultural circle' – a discussion group. The group leader would show a slide of a slum with the Spanish word for slum written at the top. The members of the group would know from their own experience what the picture was about. The group leader would try to get them talking about the slum and the way they felt about it. He would encourage them to ask questions like, 'Why are the roads not made up where we live, while the tourist areas of the town have roads that are well-maintained?' In talking about their own conditions in this way a number of things would happen. First, the members of the group would begin to bring up to the level of consciousness in their own minds their own deeply felt resentment about their conditions. Secondly, they would begin to understand why things were the way they were. Thirdly, they would begin to work out what needed to be done in order to bring about change.

While the discussion was under way, new words would be written up in front of the group, all the words having come up in conversation. Because the words had arisen from the group in the context of discussion about matters on which its members had felt deeply, they were learnt and remembered. So it could be said that in the adult education process two kinds of learning were taking place: people were learning to read and write and use and understand words, and people were learning about the social, political and economic conditions in which they were living.

## Two Voices

The name which has been given to this kind of education is 'education for liberation'. Luis Reinoso, Secretary of CELADEC (the Latin American Evangelical Commission on Christian Education), has written as follows:

> A liberating education is an education which is encompassed critically and conflictingly within the actual system. Such a form of education should be accompanied by a political revolutionary action which makes possible the advance towards an alternative society which is a truly popular democracy.

At the final gathering of the World Council of Christian Education in 1971, the Rev. Federico Pagura, Bishop of Costa Rica and Panama, said,

> The hour is coming, perhaps it is now, in which our words and our studies, our institutions and our plans, our worship and our actions, will have significance and validity, for God and the world, only in so far as they demonstrate a genuine and vital commitment to the poor of the earth, a true passion for the forgotten man, for whom Christ gave his life; this means a risking of comfort and position, tranquillity and a good name, for the living God who in Jesus Christ has made the cause of man His cause.

6. A true passion for the forgotten man?

## For Discussion

In Latin America learning to read and write goes hand in hand with acquiring political literacy, while in India it goes hand in hand with acquiring agricultural literacy. Does this suggest that learning to read and write must generally be done in relation to some practical purpose? What are the things that motivate people to become literate in western Europe and North America? Latin American adult education seems to be directed towards bringing about change in society. Is this manipulative in an unacceptable way? Is there any education which is so neutral that it does not manipulate people either in the direction of change or in the direction of accepting things as they are?

## AFRICA

In May 1974 a major international conference was held in Tanzania. It was sponsored by the Institute of Development Studies of the University of Dar es Salaam and the Dag Hammarskjöld Foundation of Sweden. (Dag Hammarskjöld was a former Secretary General of the United Nations.) It brought together 42 participants from 18 countries, 13 of them being black African nations.

One may ask why the gathering was considered to be necessary. During the fifties and sixties when most of the black African nations gained their independence, they committed a great deal of public expenditure to their educational systems. These were generally copies of the British and French systems which had been established during the colonial era and which had been considered the best in the world. Much had been hoped for from the primary and secondary schools and from the universities which had been set up. But alarmingly mass education had brought new problems. It was clear that a traditional European education was not turning out to be as helpful to the continuing development of the African nations as had been hoped. It did not equip the nations' citizens for life and the necessary work in their communities. The conference delegates hoped that as a result of conferring together they would each begin to see new ways in which their own schools, universities and informal education organizations might be developed in order to meet the needs of their people in more effective ways.

The gathering was held in Tanzania because that nation is generally regarded as being one of the first to recognize the problems involved in transplanting a European educational organization into an African culture. There has been a great deal of experimentation in the country attempting to devise educational alternatives more appropriate to its citizens, and a massive and very successful attempt to bring literacy to the population. So the conference delegates came to Dar es Salaam, talked about and analysed the educational systems in Africa, looked at educational projects in Tanzania and Zanzibar, and attempted to draw up specific suggestions for the future.

President Julius Nyerere gave the opening address of the conference, and his speech is seen as being one of the most perceptive and visionary statements on education by a national leader during the last ten years. Listening to the Tanzanian President expound his educational philosophy, the delegates at the conference began to understand why it was that his nation had made such progress in adapting its existing educational system to meet the real needs of its people.

Here is an abbreviated version of that address:

We know that something called 'education' is a good thing. And all African states therefore spend a large proportion of government revenue on it. But, I suspect that for us in Africa the underlying purpose of education is to turn us into black Europeans, or black Americans, because our education policies make it quite clear that we are really expecting education in Africa to enable us to emulate the material achievements of Europe and America. We have not begun to think seriously about whether such material achievements are possible or desirable.

The primary purpose of education is the liberation of man. To 'liberate' is to 'set free'. It implies impediments to freedom having been thrown off. But a man can be physically free from restraint and still be unfree if his mind is restricted by habits and attitudes which limit his humanity.

Education is incomplete if it enables man to work out elaborate schemes for universal peace but does not teach him how to provide good food for himself and his family. It is equally incomplete if it teaches man to be an efficient tool user and tool maker, but neglects his personality and his relationship with his fellow human being.

There are professional men who say, 'My market value is higher than the salary I am receiving in Tanzania.' But no human being has a market value — except a slave. When people say such things, in effect they are saying: 'This education I have been given has turned me into a marketable commodity, like cotton or sisal'; and they are showing that instead of liberating their humanity by giving it a greater chance to express itself, the education they have received has degraded their humanity. Their education has converted them into objects — repositories of knowledge like rather special computers.

We condemn such people. Yet it is our educational system which is instilling in boys and girls the idea that their education confers a price tag on them — which ignores the infinite and priceless value of a liberated human being, who is co-operating with others in building a civilization worthy of creatures made in the image of God.

A formal school system, devised and operated without reference to the society in which its graduates will live, is of little use as an instrument of liberation for the people of Africa. At the same time, learning just by living and doing in the existing society would leave us so backward socially and technologically that human liberation in the foreseeable future is out of the question. Somehow we have to combine the two systems. We have to integrate formal education with the society and use education as a catalyst for change in that society.

Inevitably it takes time to change. We have not solved the problem of building sufficient self-confidence to refuse what we regard as the world's best (whatever that may mean), and to choose instead the most appropriate for our conditions. We have not solved the problem of our apparent inability to integrate education and life, and education and production. We have not solved the problem of overcoming the belief that academic ability marks out a child or an adult as especially praiseworthy, or as deserving a privileged place in society.

This is not a failure within the formal education system. It is a failure of the society as a whole. Indeed, the educationalists have advanced in these matters more than other sections of the community. We have downgraded examination results in selecting pupils for secondary school; we have included course work assessment in degree awards. But our society has not yet accepted that character, co-operativeness and a desire to serve are relevant to a person's ability to benefit from further training.

At the consultation in Bergen in May 1970, organized by the World Council of Churches, Mr. Anza Lema, headmaster of the Lutheran Senior School and Junior College in Arusha, described some of the things done in his school:

> The policy of 'education for self-reliance' is based on the recognition that Tanzania has basically an agricultural economy and that its people have accepted the challenge to live and work in the spirit of *ujamaa* (socialism). Its purpose is to make education an integral part of life as pupils know it now and will have to live it in the future. Primary and secondary schools must not simply be an academic preparation for further studies, but they must prepare people for life and service in the villages and rural areas of our country.

> Since 1967, 'education for self-reliance' has been implemented in schools in Tanzania through such projects as growing vegetables on land belonging to the school, raising poultry and cattle, upkeep of school buildings and grounds by the pupils themselves, making and repairing teaching equipment (e.g. bookbinding, apparatus for physics), and participation in self-help projects of the community in which the school is situated.

The educational values of this method were threefold: first, it fostered in pupils a sense of living and working for the common good of all; secondly,

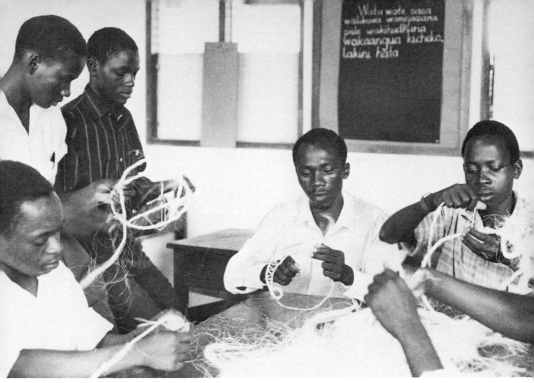

7. Sisal, a local product, is used at St. Andrew's
Teacher Training College in Korogwe, Tanzania.

it ensured that the skills taught were relevant to the practical needs of the
people; and thirdly, it ensured that pupils, by their work, contributed to the
cost of their education.

## For Discussion

What elements in President Nyerere's views about education seem strongly
influenced by a Christian view of man?

If an educational system is to change, how important is it that political
leaders and educationalists work together? What are some of the dangers in
this?

President Nyerere implies that western education focuses too much attention on the individual alone and insufficient attention on the individual
as a member of a community. How far is this true? In education is there a
conflict between co-operation and competition? How far should education
concern itself with helping to develop skills related to the life that it is most
likely that pupils will have to live, and how far with other skills which
would enable pupils to live totally different lives in new environments?

27

# 2

## PROBLEMS AND ISSUES

**Adult Illiteracy Rates in 1960 and 1970**

| Major Regions | Illiteracy (percentage) | |
|---|---|---|
| | 1960 | 1970 |
| World | 39.3 | 34.2 |
| Africa | 81.0 | 73.7 |
| North America | 2.4 | 1.5 |
| Latin America | 32.5 | 23.6 |
| Asia | 55.2 | 46.8 |
| Europe & USSR | 5.3 | 3.6 |

Illiteracy rates are calculated on the basis of the estimated number of illiterate persons aged fifteen years and over as a percentage of the total population in that age group.

*Source:* **Unesco Office of Statistics**

This table illustrates one side of the problem: two major regions of the world have extremely low illiteracy rates. These regions contain less than one-third of the world's population. Three major regions (containing more than two-thirds of the world's population) have high rates of illiteracy. To put it at its extreme, a comparison between one thousand people in each of two continents would look like this: in North America only 15 would be illiterate, while in Africa the number would be 737.

The second table illustrates the other side of the problem: to banish illiteracy costs money. Where is that money to be found? If money is spent on education, then it cannot be spent on other things, like technological investment.

## Public Expenditure on Education in 1968

| Country | As percentage of GNP[4] | As percentage of total public expenditure |
|---|---|---|
| Argentina | 2.0 | 21.0 |
| Bolivia | 3.2 | 26.1 |
| Brazil | 3.0[1] | 13.0 |
| Chile[2] | 4.6 | 10.6 |
| Costa Rica | 5.7 | 34.1 |
| West Germany | 3.5 | 10.9 |
| Ghana | 3.9 | 18.7 |
| Israel | 6.8 | 11.2 |
| Japan | 4.0 | 20.8 |
| Panama | 4.8 | 30.9 |
| Sweden | 7.9 | 26.9 |
| UK[3] | 5.6 | 12.3 |
| USA | 5.8 | 16.6 |

Notes: [1] Estimated.

[2] The proportions shown relate to 1969 expenditure.

[3] The proportions shown relate to 1967 expenditure.

[4] GNP is Gross National Product — the total value of goods and services produced by a nation in a given year.

*Source: Unesco Office of Statistics*

A number of important conclusions can be drawn from these statistics. First, the developing nations are able to spend only a significantly lower proportion of their national income on education as compared with the developed nations of western Europe and North America. Secondly, where the developing nations have succeeded in bringing their educational expenditure as a proportion of GNP towards the percentages that apply in the developed nations (e.g. Costa Rica), that expenditure has had to come from central government sources, the implications being that there was that much less money available for other needs like health and social security.

So the developing nations have to decide on priorities. It has traditionally been assumed that educational expenditure was one of the most important because it was an investment in the future: it was assumed that if a nation educated its children, then that nation would in a few years have a ready supply of educated manpower to develop its technology and industry. The trouble is that this theory has recently been called into question. It is known, for instance, that Sweden has one of the most advanced societies in the western world, and the proportion of its national income devoted to education is one of the highest in the world. But, West Germany has also become one of the most advanced and prosperous nations in the western world, and its expenditure on education as a proportion of national income is relatively low — as low as many third world nations. Does educational expenditure, therefore, really bring prosperity to a nation?

The answer is yes, of course, provided that that expenditure is on the right kind of education. It is at this point that we find ourselves right at the heart of the debate about education: what kind of education is best for different regions of the world and for different nations within those regions?

Let us return to some statements of the purposes of education that we have already considered. Newman argued that it was one of the functions of a complete education to produce a person who was a gentleman — a person with a 'cultivated intellect, a delicate taste'. Macaulay spoke of the function of education in India as being to produce 'a class of persons Indian in blood and colour, but English in taste, opinions, in morals and intellect'. President Nyerere, in criticizing the traditional education provided in the newly independent African nations, did so on the grounds that its purpose appeared to be to turn Africans into black Europeans or black Americans.

Educationalists in the developing nations of the third world have now recognized that a traditional western style education will not of itself solve their problems; on the contrary, it may make them worse. In the last decade a great deal of criticism has been levelled against the systems of education which western Europe and North America transplanted on to the cultures of Asia, Africa and Latin America during the last hundred years. The hope has been that through such criticism it would be possible to devise alternative systems which would be better able to meet the needs of their people.

## Some of the Issues
It has been argued that one of the most serious consequences of schooling, particularly in Africa, is that it has gone hand in hand with urbanization: as a nation became industrialized, the schooling in the villages took children off the land and away from their homes. One of its unfortunate results was that children who had learned how to read and write began to look down on their homes and villages where few of the adults were literate. They became dissatisfied, and longed for the glittering rewards to be found in the big towns — rewards promised them by the advertisements that they were now able to read and understand.

8. On the pavement outside Grant Road Station in Bombay.

So the young school leavers left the villages and moved to the towns where they hoped to earn a great deal of money, in order to enjoy the freedom of independence. When they arrived there, they found it wasn't like that at all. There were more people wanting jobs in the towns than there was work available; there were insufficient housing and accommodation to cater for those already trying to live in the towns, without having to find room for others wishing to come in; and, as always in heavily populated areas, there were people ready to exploit the young boys and girls coming from sheltered village communities.

Schooling cannot be blamed for the problems of urbanization, but it did reinforce a process which had been begun, and accentuate its problems. To refer once again to President Nyerere's speech, western education has encouraged Africans to think that they were able to use their education to demand more from society than they were prepared to give. The President maintained that education had thus turned them from human beings into marketable commodities.

A related problem is that which has to do with a person's need to maintain contacts with his historical roots. In a traditional African village, the history and the myths of the community would be handed down from generation to generation through the telling of stories. In this way African culture and its rich heritage were kept alive. A European-style education said implicitly to the African child, 'The things that you do in your village communities are primitive and of a bygone age; the things that you need to learn to do are the things which your European teachers tell you.' So African children were taught to sing English hymns, say English prayers and learn English customs and habits, and even wear European clothes. Conditioning African children to believe that their own culture was bad and that European and American values were good made them susceptible to the advertisers who could promise them all the frills of western society.

The Latin American critics of western education regard this as exploitation directed towards expanding the export markets of the western industrialized economies. Many of them would not go as far as to maintain that it is deliberately organized in this way — they simply argue that this is one of the indirect consequences of western schooling: if a developing nation adopts the educational system of an advanced economy, then it is inevitable that its children will adopt the values of that advanced economy, and wish to have the things that it offers. Thus, although many nations of the third world have gained their political independence in the last twenty years, they still remain economically dependent upon the advanced industrialized nations of the west.

The challenge facing the developing nations is that they must clearly progress technologically, but they must do this without losing their identities. Therefore they must not take wholesale the blueprints for progress spelt out by the western world. They must discover for themselves a way of progressing which is most appropriate to their cultures. The Shakespeare a European may value so highly may not be appropriate for an African.

Some of the struggles relating to education in various parts of the world represent an attempt to shake off what are regarded as the shackles of a western understanding of education and society, in order to discover new and appropriate educational systems for developing nations.

## Some Key Words and Phrases

*Intermediate Technology*
The person who made this phrase famous was the economist Dr. E. F. Schumacher. His most well-known book in which he spelt out what he meant by intermediate technology was *Small is Beautiful.* In this book he has a pointed illustration, relating to the needs of India. Schumacher argues that if people are unemployed, a country is wasting its economic resources. One of the major problems facing the Indian subcontinent is to create employment for all its people. This leads to the basic question, 'What is education for?' He quotes a Chinese calculation that it took the work of thirty peasants to keep one man or woman at a university. If that person took a five-year course he would have consumed 150 peasant-work years. And what would he do with that education which he had been given? He would move into a fashionable district of Bombay where many other highly educated people lived and where he could join 'a mutual admiration society' − a 'trade union of the privileged' − to see to it that his privileges were not eroded by the great masses of his contemporaries who had not been educated. Such an education was wrong. The only education which was right was one which took the educated person back to the people whose work had paid for his education in order that he could repay them with interest for the benefit of the community as a whole. How could he repay them? By using his knowledge to create employment.

However, creating jobs requires investment. Schumacher estimated that over a ten-year period India would have approximately £7,500 million for the creation of jobs. If setting up a job cost £150 per work place, then you could create 50 million jobs in that period. While if setting up a job cost £5,000 per work place, then you could create only about 1·7 million jobs in that period. The capital required to provide the tools for a man to do a basic

33

agricultural job was £150. The capital required to create a job in a high technology industry (like a car factory) was £10,000 per man. So he asks, 'What makes us think we need electricity, cement and steel before we can do anything at all?' He argues that one should give people the tools to do basic essential jobs efficiently and teach them how to use those tools; then everybody will be productively employed, the economy will grow, and the nation will be able to afford high technological industries when it is ready for them.

This is a simplified statement of his case. When fully worked out it does take account of a whole range of complex economic factors, and he claims that it can be applied in all developing economies. He makes a specific suggestion in relation to India:

> Suppose you were to make it obligatory for every able-bodied person in India to plant and see to the establishment of one tree a year, five years running. This, in a five-year period, would give you 2,000 million established trees. Anyone can work it out on the back of an envelope that the economic value of such an enterprise, intelligently conducted, would be greater than anything that has ever been promised by any of India's five-year plans. It could be done without a penny of foreign aid; there is no problem of savings and investment. It would produce foodstuffs, fibres, building materials, shade, water, almost anything that man really needs . . . I ask, what sort of an education is it that prevents us from thinking of things ready to be done immediately?

The principle behind the theory of intermediate technology is that it is no use investing in a technology whose products cannot be afforded by the community. For instance, it is no use building a car factory in a country where no one can afford a car — unless you can sell it abroad more cheaply than anyone else and in return buy something that the population can afford. This principle applies also in the advanced western economies, and its implication is that the growth of technology must be related to the needs of the national community, and education must be directed towards helping a people to use its appropriate technology.

*Functional Literacy*
The former Director-General of UNESCO, René Maheu, has said of adult education that it

> contributes to development more directly and speedily than any form of education, since the adults are, by definition, the most active agents of development. To make illiterate adults literate is a prime condition for the general progress of the society because of the immediate increase in human potential which it brings about.

34

But he was quick to point out that literacy did not simply mean being able to read and write. Nor did it have anything to do with cramming a pupil's head full of information which did not appear to be relevant to him in the society in which he would have to live out his life — there was thus not much point in teaching an African child about the kings and queens of England, nor a Brazilian child about George Washington.

Intermedia, an international organization concerned with literacy education, has suggested that for a person to be functionally literate the following conditions should exist:

1. He should be able to read critically and understand manufacturers' instruction sheets, be able to write a letter to a government office requesting information, and be able to understand measurements like land areas, seed quantities, interest charges and rent.

2. He should have an elementary understanding of the processes of nature in relation to health and sanitation, to raising crops and animals, to nutrition, food storage and preparation, and to the environment and its protection.

3. He should know how to run a household, including the protection of family health, caring for injured and sick, intelligently using money, making clothes, doing household repairs, and growing and preserving food.

4. He should have the knowledge and skills to make a living.

5. He should have the knowledge and skills to participate in the life of the community through political and social activities.

6. He should have an image of himself as a person who can learn and who in co-operation with family and fellow citizens can participate fully and creatively in the life of society.

*Hidden Curriculum*
In any educational programme there are two kinds of curriculum. There is the curriculum that we can know and identify: the mathematical ideas that a teacher is trying to transmit to his pupils, the historical and geographical knowledge that a pupil is trying to learn, the musical and recreational skills whose development a teacher is trying to encourage in a pupil. When we say that a pupil is attending a French lesson we know that the curriculum in that classroom will be directed towards helping him learn to understand the French language.

But there is another kind of curriculum in every educational situation. It is called the hidden curriculum, because those involved may not be aware of it. It is the name given to the values which are transmitted implicitly rather than explicitly. For instance, an educational system in which pupils have to sit competitive examinations regularly, in which they are graded by being given positions in class (like 1st, 10th, last), in which they are frequently given tests where they must not help one another, and in which there is considerable emphasis on competitive sport — such an educational system transmits the lesson that competition is a good and normal part of social living and is to be encouraged. Many people in western societies find it almost impossible to question fundamentally the competitive assumptions of their environment because they have been so thoroughly and effectively conditioned to accept those assumptions, assumptions which were transmitted to them without their realizing or choosing, partly through the hidden curriculum of their education.

The danger of the hidden curriculum is that most of us are unaware of it and we therefore have little choice in the matter. It is a kind of conditioning or, to use a more loaded phrase, a kind of brainwashing.

It is generally thought that part of the hidden curriculum of education is the transmission of the idea that intellectual ability is superior to manual ability, the idea that it is better to compete than to co-operate, the idea that to be an individual is more important than to be a member of a community, the idea that to be white is somehow better than to be black. It is also maintained that the hidden curriculum of educational institutions generally reinforces the existing power structures in society — parents, police, the law, teachers, and what we might generally call the economic and social system. That is why those most concerned to change the conditions of the underprivileged in the world regard it as fundamental to expose the values of the hidden curriculum and to substitute alternatives.

*Domestication and Liberation*
These two words are frequently set in opposition to one another. Paulo Freire has said that an educational system will either liberate or it will domesticate: it must do one or the other. It can never be neutral.

The word 'domesticate' is used to describe a subtle conditioning process in which a person is led to accept the conditions in which he finds himself and to believe that there is little he can do about them. Many of the values which lead to domestication are transmitted through the hidden curriculum. It is as a result of this conditioning that many people place a low value upon themselves. Thus if, in an educational system which they were taught to regard as having authority, they were continually being told that they

**EDUCATION PERMANENTE**

9. The power of the hidden curriculum.

were no good (through having always been given low marks, through rarely having been given credit for effort, through usually having been involved in the courses which were referred to as being for the 'less able'), they would naturally leave school with feelings of inferiority and worthlessness.

A domesticating education was one which could allow people to succeed and flourish only within fairly rigid frameworks. Traditional schooling in most countries in the world is generally regarded by advanced educationalists as being domesticating because the range of gifts whose development it will encourage is strictly limited. It will tend to allow only academic gifts to flourish. It will tend to reinforce the gifts of those in society who are already relatively privileged (and who will for that reason not wish to bring about changes in the structure of society). It will tend to devalue the strengths of those in society who are relatively underprivileged (and when people are devalued they lose the motivation to bring about change). It will tend to help society exploit the weak for the benefit of the strong (e.g. through high pressure advertising).

A liberating education on the other hand makes a person believe in himself. It asserts that however oppressed a person may be he is still a human being of infinite worth. It makes him aware not so much of his weaknesses but of his strengths. It gives him confidence in himself, and helps him to discover how he can take responsibility for his own life. It shows him that he is not simply the victim of circumstances, but assures him that he has power over his own destiny. It shows him that he is a creative human being who has something to contribute, with others, to the benefit of mankind as a whole.

A domesticating education is concerned with conformity, resistance to change, individuality and competitiveness; a liberating education is concerned with creativity, change in society, with community and co-operation.

*Conscientization*

This is a word which has been invented to encapsulate the objectives of a liberating education. Conscientization involves a person's becoming aware of the ways in which he is oppressed by the structures of society, becoming aware of what he needs to do in order to change things, and having the self-confidence to act.

The first task is to raise people's awareness of the hidden values in a community or in society. Things are rarely as they seem to be. When a person living in a slum area of a Latin American city accepts his condition, apparently without question, the adult educator will encourage him to ask questions. Why does he accept that he must live in a slum while others live in luxury apartments? He might answer that they are better than he is. But why does he think that — is it not because he has been conditioned to believe it from his earliest childhood? When he becomes aware of the conditioning that has moulded his attitudes he can then face himself realistically, and through being given opportunities to be creative he can arrive at a new valuation of himself. He can see himself as an oppressed member of a society in which there are oppressors and oppressed (two more significant words in the armoury of the third world adult educator). He learns how to identify who the oppressors are (those who in a thousand subtle ways try to prevent change from occurring in society without deliberately oppressing or being aware that they are doing so) and how he is oppressed by them. He can then address himself to the task of liberating himself from oppression. Having liberated himself from the oppression of ignorance he is already on the path to liberation from the oppression of poverty. But he must work out the solutions appropriate to his condition. He can do it with others as a member of a group or community. But the members of that group must discover for themselves what are the solutions to their problems — no one outside the situation can provide the answers for them. True to the best principles of education it involves a process of discovery. And when people discover things for themselves, they gain in self-esteem and self-confidence.

## Cultural Circle
This is a kind of discussion group (*circulo de cultura*) in which adult literacy education takes place. Educators and learners talk together about the reason why injustice in general, and slums in particular exist. This kind of discussion is sometimes referred to as 'engaging in dialogue' because its aim is that each member of the group will try to communicate to the others how he perceives things, and through sharing one another's perceptions all (both learners and educators) will reach new insights. Each person comes to the group with an idea in his mind of why things are the way they are. We can call these ideas 'myths'. Each person has his own myth. As the group proceeds, one by one the myths are removed (e.g. the myth that a particular slum-dweller is inferior to a person living in the more prosperous part of the city) and truth is unveiled and seen for what it is.

## Education permanente
The English term for this is 'lifelong integrated learning'. It seeks to make the point that human beings spend all their lives learning, from the cradle to the

10. People of all ages need a relevant education.

grave. And yet most of the publicly provided education covers a period between a person's fifth and fifteenth birthdays. In point of fact adults are as much in need of education as are children, especially in the developing nations. But this education must be related directly to people's needs: their needs to adapt to changing social and economic circumstances. The more attention is given to meeting people's adult education needs in these terms, the more likely is a developing nation able to optimize its growth and progress.

## For Discussion

During the 1960s there was a great expansion in expenditure on education in the western economically developed nations. The early seventies saw some contraction in educational spending. This was partly due to the accompanying world economic recession. But three questions arise:

1. Was that expenditure worth while?

2. How long a time span do we need before we can be sure that we know the answer to question 1?

3. What are the likely consequences which follow from increased or reduced educational expenditure, to job expectations of young people newly on the labour market, to employment prospects and to the path of economic development?

Many of the ideas which have been considered in this chapter suggest that the only worthwhile education is in matters which are relevant to people in the immediate or short-term future — any other kind of education is a waste of money, time and energy, and does more harm than good. How true is this of education in advanced western societies? How far does education in western societies enable people to be functionally literate — i.e. enable them to function in an informed and effective way in their own societies? In what ways is functional literacy to be understood differently in different contexts?

What do you think is the hidden curriculum in the schools in your country? Compare that with the hidden curriculum in the schools of the developing countries as far as you can identify them.

Is it possible that all in any society need to have their awareness heightened of the conditioning forces within which they live, in order that change may be brought about? Could this imply that all in society (whether regarded as oppressor or oppressed) need to talk together, engage in dialogue together, so that all may together find liberation?

# 3

## INTERNAL OBSTACLES AND HINDRANCES

### The Classical Dilemma

It is generally agreed that the educational systems in developing countries face serious problems. In spite of enormous expenditure on education, the number of people in the world who are illiterate is increasing every day (though the proportion may be falling). The proportion of pupils who fail to complete courses in schools and colleges in developing countries is enormous by comparison with those failing to complete in developed nations. Education appears to bring in its wake a variety of new problems with which it apparently does not enable people and nations to cope − e.g. urbanization and unemployment.

There are two ways of looking at the problem − the classical and the radical: the classical way implies that the real problem is one of quantity and quality − we simply need to provide more of the best of traditional education; the radical way implies that there is something fundamentally wrong with the kind of education that is provided.

We shall look at each of these in turn. First, the classical approach.

There is always the problem of money: this has been referred to in an earlier section, and represents also one of the main external constraints on educational development (to be discussed in a later section). However, to refer specifically to school fees, it has for example been estimated that secondary school fees in Uganda can cost as much as 40% of the minimum wage in Kampala. When a boy goes to school, he not only costs his parents his fees and other school expenses, but he also deprives them of any income that he might earn.

There are other obstacles as well. One of the most serious is that of overcrowded classes. The average pupil/teacher ratio in schools in Africa, Asia and Latin America is between 60 and 70 to 1. Secondary school teachers in England are at present claiming that a pupil/teacher ratio of 18:1 is too high for effective education to occur. However, the developing nations know that they must try to produce indigenous teachers rather than rely on those coming from abroad. It takes several years to provide locally trained teachers. And while a nation is busy training its own educators, the school population continues to increase. Furthermore it seems that it will be destined to endure overcrowded classes for many years — at least until the growth in population is arrested.

It is often suggested that the mass media should be used for some educational work: a single radio programme can reach several million people at once. It is being tried in India, but there are two problems. First, few people in poor areas can afford radios. Secondly, even if a group of people can be assembled around a communal radio to listen to a particular programme, there is still the need for a teacher who will work with the members of the group. The radio on its own is not an adequate educational tool — it requires the support of a locally based teacher.

Many primary schools face the problem of pupils in a given age group progressing at different speeds. Some progress so slowly that it becomes necessary for them to spend a second year in the same class. This extends the length of time pupils spend in the primary schools, and increases the school population. One solution is to do what is done in Britain and the United States: to provide automatic promotion at the end of each year, so that a child never stays in the same class for two years. But in order to implement a policy such as this it becomes necessary to develop an additional structure providing classes for slow learners and other pupils with special learning difficulties. More expense.

Many critics of education in developing countries claim that there has been too much emphasis on primary education and insufficient attention given to other sectors such as technical and adult education. The result has been that primary education has attempted to teach as many young pupils as possible to read and write. But when they leave school they have no use for their reading and writing, particularly if they live in rural communities where nobody ever sees a book, let alone reads one, and there is never any reason to write a letter. It is argued that providing people with education is a waste of time unless you can at the same time provide them with the opportunities for making use of that education. Since western education is essentially related to technological progress, a western style education in

11. Cleaning pots and kettles with grass.

developing countries demands a western type of economic growth. The only way of ensuring that is to devote more resources to technical and adult education and less to primary and traditional university education. That again provides a difficult choice for political leaders to make.

The predicament facing some countries looks like this: if the quality of primary education is so poor that most pupils lapse back into illiteracy soon after leaving school (most not proceeding to secondary schools), the whole exercise has been a waste of time. Would it not therefore be better to provide a few good schools with good teachers and good equipment for a few pupils, rather than provide a mediocre education for all who want it? This is not a choice which many political leaders in any country would find easy to make.

Another difficulty arises from the fact that most education in rural areas has been predominantly confined to the primary level. Secondary education has either been restricted to urban areas, or has consisted of boarding school well away from the village environment. One of the ways of dealing with this problem is to reduce the school day in the rural communities, so that children of primary age spend less time in school, thus releasing the buildings and the teachers for work with older pupils. The problem is that they are not trained for this work, and in most cases the village communities regard older children as labour which must not be wasted. To solve this difficulty, the education provided for older pupils in these circumstances must relate to the needs of the villages. At this point the teacher finds that he needs the help of an agriculturalist.

Another problem facing schools is that the education they provide tends to be in a language which is new to the children — in African village communities it is the language of the colonial powers, and in Latin America it is sometimes regarded as the language of the invader (i.e. Portuguese or Spanish). Since these languages are those used in the wider community, it is inevitable that schools should conduct education in these tongues. But it doesn't help in making education immediately relevant to pupils.

School-leaving certificates always cause problems. Traditionally, many African and West Indian pupils took Cambridge and London General Certificate of Education examinations at Ordinary and at Advanced Level. From the early sixties the Cambridge Board attempted to encourage some of the African nations to set up local examining bodies so that the examination curriculum of pupils in African schools could be developed in a way that was most appropriate to the educational needs of the pupils. But this kind of programme is expensive to establish, and it is frequently thought to be easier and more economic to continue using British examination boards, in spite of the consequences that this will be bound to have on the school system as a whole.

A typical problem has arisen with the establishment of the Caribbean Examinations Council. It was hoped that when this council was set up it would devise new forms of assessment and syllabus suited to the region's needs. Because the council is under-financed it looks as if it will only be able to copy the existing inherited patterns.

It had been hoped that one of the consequences of the development of general education would be that, in addition to providing an educated élite to run society, it might undermine traditional hierarchies (such as the caste system in parts of India) by providing everyone with the opportunity of gaining access to that élite. While to some degree it has succeeded in this, in point of fact any existing élite will tend to recruit its successors from its own offspring — the children of the educated leaders of society will, when they enter the school system, have all the advantages, which will ensure that they come out at the top when their education is completed. So, while education has enabled a traditional social hierarchy to be eliminated, it has done so by creating another.

An educational system will inevitably reflect the values of the society in which it is set: an unjust society is unlikely to produce a fair educational system; a violent society is unlikely to produce an educational system which does not in some way do violent things to those within it. But the educational system is not simply a passive offshoot of society – it can help to bring about changes in the total community where that community wishes these changes to occur. It is generally thought that two conclusions follow from this. First, educational changes can begin to have their effect on society if they are directed towards minor social and economic improvements from which large numbers of the population are seen to benefit. Secondly, no society can develop in any new directions without there being some accompanying changes in the educational world. This is the tension, the dilemma, in which educationalists find themselves caught.

Another problem is that of educating the educators; as new and more effective and worthwhile educational methods are discovered and devised, it becomes increasingly important to provide more of what is called 'in-service training' for teachers and others. This again is expensive. But it is not only the expense that is the problem – there is the difficulty of changing the attitudes of many teachers whose training was undertaken a few years ago when the aims of education were much more clear and thought to be straightforward. In point of fact, it is usually the people most in need of in-service training who are least likely to come forward to make use of it.

## The Radical Dilemma

> My husband has read much,
> He has read extensively and deeply,
> He has read among white men
> And he is clever like white men.
>
> And the reading
> Has killed my man
> In the ways of his people,
> He has become a stump.

These lines from the poem *Song of Lawino* were written by the African poet Okot P'Bitek and published in 1966 by the East Africa Publishing

46

House. They describe the feelings of an African woman about what her husband's education has done to him. 'The author, a Makerere lecturer, was writing of what western education had done to his society; a song of protest and lament put into the mouth of an Acoli girl who had been wrenched from her traditional life to be the wife of an educated man living in the modern city of Kampala.' So writes Gwen Cashmore in *The Broken Circle*, an unpublished paper being 'a study of the idea of self-hood in African society, with particular reference to an imported school system'.

Working in a training college in Uganda, Gwen Cashmore tried to find out if there was any fundamental difference between the way in which the western teachers understood themselves and the way in which the African students understood themselves. She saw a clear difference, and showed it diagrammatically like this:

**Western Concepts of Self-hood**

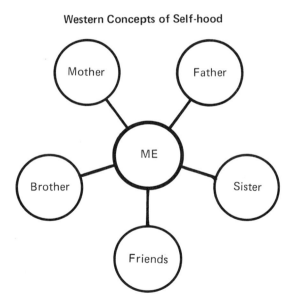

The western teacher understood himself as an individual who was related to other people, but the people to whom he felt himself to be related could be changed: he could switch his friends. If he disliked his relatives, he could cut them out of his life without feeling any sense of loss.

## African Concepts of Self-hood

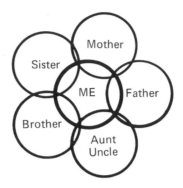

The African student always saw himself as part of his family and his village and community. He could never see himself as isolated from them. As one student put it: 'I am never alone. I am always Monica Mugume, the daughter of Mpendwaki, the grand-daughter of . . . , the sister of . . .' Thus the death of one member of the family was felt as deeply as if it were the death of a part of oneself.

In addition to this, John Taylor, in *The Primal Vision*, points out the ways in which the traditional culture of Africa enables a person not only to feel that he is a part of his relatives and community, but also that he and nature are at one: he is harmoniously a part of the totality of creation. The natural order does not have to be fought against but lived with.

R. H. Tawney, in *Religion and the Rise of Capitalism*, shows that western man saw life in the same way until the coming of the Reformation. Until that time Europe was a close-knit society of small communities. A child was born into a community to which he belonged — a community which would care for him and to which he owed responsibilities. He did not have to earn his value — it was his birthright.

The Reformation changed all this. Calvinism proclaimed the uniqueness of the individual before God, and consequently the responsibility of each person for his own soul. 'Thus there arose a concept of separateness, of individual self-hood: of a spiritual aloneness and responsibility for the destiny of one's own soul.' (Cashmore, *ibid.*)

While the Reformation gave man a sense of spiritual aloneness, the industrial revolution made man physically alone: people moved to the towns and cities and became physically separated from their communities. Man became a city dweller, cut off from his wider family and his roots in the land.

Tawney argues that Calvinism, with its doctrine of material rewards as a sign of God's blessing, set loose a drive for power and wealth from which the west is still suffering. Eric Fromm, in *Escape from Freedom*, supports his thesis and goes on to claim that western man is today suffering the consequences of that movement which began five centuries ago: he claims that western man feels isolated, alienated from himself, his fellow human beings, and his environment: he feels himself rootless, and is therefore at the mercy of the competitive-achieving ethic which dominates society and by which he is valued.

When European missionaries first went to Africa, they took with them the values which had become part of their own cultures. They set up educational systems based on those assumptions. At the time they thought they were doing what was best for Africa. They thought they were proclaiming the Christian gospel, and transmitting to Africa all the good things which were the product of a Christian heritage. What they did not realize was that they set Africa off on the same path which Europe had begun to tread a couple of centuries earlier. It has taken western man three or four centuries to reach the point where he asks seriously where all this technology, urbanization and affluence is leading.

Many people in Africa have quite quickly come to the realization that that continent cannot go in the same direction as western society without African man paying the terrible price of losing his intrinsic cultural identity, i.e. losing his essential African-ness. If he goes in the same direction as the west, he will simply become a black European. The result will be that some precious insights about the nature of man, which many in Africa still perceive but which the west has largely lost, will be lost to mankind as a whole.

There is a story told of a young boy in an African village:

A nurse from the nearby mission came to visit a boy's mother when she was ill. The nurse noticed that the boy seemed unusually bright, and as a result suggested to the parents that he should be sent to school. At first the parents couldn't understand why their son needed to go to school — he was already learning in the family and the village all that he would need to know to help his father in the fields and to play his part in the life of the village community. The nurse, however, was persuasive: the boy had talent; if he did well at school he could join the civil service and become a great leader of his nation. The parents relented, and the boy went to school.

He did very well. He soon became top of his class, and when the time came to leave the primary school, there was no doubt that he should go on to the secondary school on the hill a few miles outside the village. It was expensive: there were school fees to be found, there were school uniform and books and pencils to be bought. But he was the first boy from his village ever to reach the secondary school. The whole village was proud of him. Since his own family could not afford to pay for his education themselves, other people in the village helped out. It was not long before the whole village had an emotional investment in him doing well at school.

The boy would come home for his holidays, but boarding school education helped the boy to grow away from his family; he lost interest in helping his father in the fields. He lost interest in village life. He was no longer part of that community. He took his secondary school examinations (General Certificate of Education, Cambridge Board) and passed with flying colours. So he went to the university. Eventually he was awarded his degree, and went to work in the civil service. He had an office in the centre of Nairobi, and a large apartment in one of its suburbs.

Three years later, he bought himself a Mercedes car, and decided that he would go and visit his family. He drove back to his village in his new car, wearing his new western-style clothes. He could not get the car right up to the village because the road was not properly made up. He walked the remainder of the distance, and told all the villagers about this wonderful machine that could carry a man at great speed from one end of the country to the other, and they all came out to see the car. They stood around, admiring it, touching it with reverence: for them the car became the symbolic prize for all the emotional and financial investment which the village had placed on the boy.

This boy has now become part of the power structure of his nation. As a leading civil servant he has all the good things which an affluent society can provide. He has the chance to travel abroad — to go to Europe and America. He can see for himself the relative wealth and luxury of those societies, and he compares these with the village life that he once knew. Because he himself has moved from life in the village to the experience of life in advanced western societies, he cannot be critical of what he can only regard as progress. He won't want things to change in his society. He wants more people in Kenya to be educated in order that more people may have the chance of experiencing the benefits of affluence. He is grateful to the educational system through which he went, and he wants his government to spend more money on that same kind of education so that others may benefit.

His village doesn't want things to be any different either: they invested all their hopes in this boy, and he fulfilled all their greatest aspirations. His success is their success. They feel that they share his triumph. They cannot understand why people want to change this educational system which has enabled them to touch this magnificent silent machine that can enable their protégé to move swiftly from the village to the big city that he may lead his nation to a better future.

If the men with power don't want things to be any different, and if the people who are potentially the consumers don't want things to be any different, what hope is there that change can be brought about? Very little. And here lies the greatest obstacle to the reform of the educational systems of Africa: the civil service and industry offer lucrative posts to graduates; the universities, based on their European counterparts, offer the passports to these posts and therefore implicitly control the curricula of secondary schools, which in turn control the curricula of primary schools, which basically most people approve of because nearly every village will have its success story of a boy who benefited, on their behalf, from that traditional European education.

Of course, for every success story, there are plenty of stories of failure: for every boy who fulfilled his parents' dreams there are many who went to the big city in search of jobs and success, and who could not find work, and who turned to crime, went to prison, or moved into the slums and lost contact with their homes. The village forgets about them (even though their parents don't). But they are becoming an increasing problem, and the more perceptive of the political leaders know that there must be changes.

But creative change needs a reasonably settled environment. If there are constant changes of leadership and power in a nation, people will all too easily blame the government for the things that are wrong in society, rather than the system which the government is required to administer — a system which basically the people themselves don't want changed. But as unemployment and poverty increase, more and more people become dissatisfied, and willing to join an army and follow a leader who will offer them dreams of success.

African nations need settled governments that are respected by the people, with leaders aware of the social problems which industrialization has brought, and leaders who are having some success in solving those problems. Tanzania is an example of such a nation. And while it attempts to solve the problems of the big cities, it also sets about trying to change the educational system in a way which is seen to be helpful to the people of the land: moving in a direction that takes account of traditional African insights (like the importance of the community and co-operation, the family, the village and agriculture) and yet is seen to be of benefit to everyone and not only to those who through educational success can move to the towns.

But even President Nyerere reminds us that there are still far too many people in his country who do not understand what he is trying to do in

12. The fruits of an affluent society.

reforming the educational system, and there are still far too many people opposed to his educational reforms. So he is not as confident as he would like to be of the successful implementation of his changes.

## For Discussion

Here are some more lines from the poem quoted at the beginning of the last section:

> And he endlessly
> Drummed his meaningless words
> Through his blocked nose,
> And we shouted the words back at him,
> And the moonlight dance-drums
> Thundered in the distance
> And the songs came floating
> From beyond his hills.
>
> The girls are dancing
> Before their lovers
> Shaking their waists
> To the rhythm of the drums
> And I
> Sitting like stale bread
> On the rubbish heap . . .

How difficult is it for those who have experienced the fruits of an affluent society, and found them empty and unsatisfying, to convince those who have not yet experienced them that they are not worth having? How can people be helped to discriminate between those fruits of technological progress which are good and those which are likely to be bad?

Education as we have known it through all the forms of society which have lasted for any length of time has been the select instrument by means of which existing values and balances of power have been maintained and kept in effect, with all the implications of both a positive and negative character which this process has had for the destiny of nations and the course of history.
(*Learning To Be: The World of Education Today and Tomorrow*, by Edgar Faure, on behalf of UNESCO, 1972.)

# 4

## EXTERNAL OBSTACLES AND HINDRANCES

### Money

All education costs money: between 1961 and 1967 the average rates of increase in expenditure on education were: Africa 45%, Latin America 45%, Asia 42%. The world's average increase was 32%. The developing countries were being encouraged by the United Nations to maintain this above average rate of increase in educational expenditure at least to 1980. In a previous chapter we have looked at the implications of this. The important thing to remember is that the developing nations can only increase their expenditure on education in a context of world economic growth.

The early seventies saw a major world economic recession. During a world recession the developing countries are particularly vulnerable. They are the major producers of the primary products which the developed nations require for manufacturing and other industries. But it is the prices of these which fluctuate most during the world economic cycle. No nation can embark with confidence on a programme of educational expansion unless it can be assured of an accompanying growth in its national income over the period.

Many educational innovations which were started in developing nations as the world was approaching the peak of an economic cycle have found themselves abandoned a couple of years later because the subsequent collapse in world commodity prices meant that there was not the cash to sustain them.

## Mobility

One of the consequences of the establishment of a system of higher education is that its graduates become internationally mobile: in their universities the students will meet lecturers from other nations, and they will be encouraged to travel abroad. Sometimes it is suggested that spending a certain amount of time studying in another country will enhance their education still further. But there is always the possibility that once they have left the country they will not return.

Two illustrations of what has happened are appropriate here. First, it is frequently said that the British National Health Service would collapse if all the Indian doctors in Britain were to leave. India needs doctors, but so does Britain. And it is relatively easy for Britain to encourage Indian doctors to continue to work within its Health Service.

Secondly, the London School of Economics has traditionally been the institution of higher education in Britain providing courses in economics and political science which most attracted students from Africa. The majority of African students attending the LSE have returned to their homelands, and many have taken senior political and civil service posts as a result. This has generally been regarded as an illustration of the way in which the establishment in developing nations of universities of a sufficiently high academic standard (by western values) made it possible for their graduates to benefit (on behalf of the nation as a whole) from a period of study abroad. But, by implication, the universities of the developed world set the standards which the third world nations feel they must copy if their students are to have any chance in the international graduate market. If the external world determines the standards, it also determines the structures and the curricula. So, however much the nations of the third world wish to change their educational systems, they are hamstrung by their need to provide higher education comparable to that available in other nations.

## Language

One of the difficulties encountered by international agencies trying to give support to new innovations in education in developing countries arises from the fact that a new language has to be used in order to communicate the new ideas. Agencies like the World Council of Churches, UNESCO, the Commission on the Churches' Participation in Development, and others, find themselves having to use words like liberation and domestication, conscientization, oppressed, marginal citizen, functional literacy, hidden curriculum, lifelong learning, and so on. When they use such words, they are immediately criticized by many in the west with whom they must communicate in order to maintain support. Their critics label these words 'jargon' and reject the ideas that they seek to convey. They will not concede the truth of what the Latin American radical educationalists say about language, namely that it is a powerful weapon of oppression: by determining which words can be used in any discussion it is possible to control the ideas which will be allowed expression in that debate. Only by forcing the language — introducing new words, or investing traditional words with new meanings — does it become possible for new ideas to emerge. The British, because they regard the English language as their own, find it particularly difficult to come to terms with other people using it in new ways. International agencies find their financial support, and therefore their work, frequently threatened when they try to express to the west the ideas and insights which emerge from the developing world.

## Political and Economic Factors

International agencies like UNESCO receive large proportions of their funding from the western powers like the United States. Because these agencies are dependent upon the western powers, they can bring strong influence to bear upon decisions as to which countries are to receive educational aid, and the precise nature of the aid which is provided. Two illustrations can bear this out.

First, in 1976 the United States threatened to withhold its subscriptions to UNESCO until that organization dropped from its programme projects designed for Palestinian refugees. The Americans described their stand as an act of solidarity with Israel.

Secondly, since the World Council of Churches established its Programme to Combat Racism (some of whose funds have been used for educational purposes by revolutionary organizations), a small but vocal minority of Christians in various parts of Europe have attempted to bring to their church synods resolutions calling upon their churches to withhold some part of their subscription to the WCC. In a few cases they have succeeded.

It is also said that some of those nations in the developing world which are important to the United States for political, economic or strategic reasons will find their financial support from America threatened if they allow their educational systems to develop in radical directions. It is difficult to prove this, but it is logical to assume that the American government would soon bring political pressure to bear on allied nations which began to develop an educational system through which the values of the free world as America understood them were subjected to serious questioning.

It is also sometimes said that the large multi-national corporations — the big international companies — exercise a powerful influence on the nations of the developing world. In some instances they appear to have more power than many governments. Some small countries, particularly some of the island nations in the West Indies and in south-east Asia, are particularly vulnerable. If all that they have to offer the world in economic terms in order to survive is deep-water harbours, and if these are required by the international oil companies, the sensible thing to do is to come to some mutually beneficial arrangement. One of the consequences of such an arrangement in which a small nation effectively becomes economically dependent upon a large foreign-controlled company is that a whole country can effectively sell its soul. Its educational system will be directed towards teaching people the skills which the foreign-owned company requires and the habits of life which western man has taught himself to believe to be good.

## For Discussion

How did you react to the words and phrases used earlier in this book? Was your immediate reaction to regard them as meaningless jargon? To what extent is jargon the technical language of ideas that are new? How important is it for the nations of the developing world that people in western Europe and North America should think critically about their own educational systems?

# 5

## AGENCIES AND INDIVIDUALS

### The World Council of Churches

The World Council of Churches (WCC) was formed in 1948 at an assembly held in Amsterdam. It was the practical outcome of a number of ecumenical gatherings going back to a conference held in Edinburgh in 1910. Although the WCC worked without an education unit in its early years, the subject of education appeared on its agenda on many occasions, as it had done on the agendas of the various ecumenical conferences. So the New Delhi Assembly in 1961 called for a Joint Study Commission on Education to be set up and to report to the next assembly at Uppsala, Sweden, in 1968. The commission met, talked, consulted the member churches of the WCC, and prepared a report which was considered at great length at Uppsala. The assembly came to the decision that education was so important an issue that the council had to set up its own education unit. The questions posed by education all over the world were of such importance that the WCC had to establish a professionally competent unit to help the member churches understand the issues which were at stake.

In the original unit, three areas of work were considered to be those which warranted the appointment of specialist staff; general education (schools, universities, adult education), Christian education (Sunday schools, church education programmes), and theological education. When the unit was originally established, it was specifically charged with instructions that it keep in close contact with other educational bodies that existed at that time, such as UNESCO, the International Labour Office, the World Council of Christian Education, the Theological Education Fund, and the World Student Christian Federation.

The first major activity of the unit was the holding of the consultation on the 'World Educational Crisis and the Church's Contribution' at Bergen, Holland, in May 1970. The purposes of the consultation were:

- to attempt to see education whole
- to learn about educational innovations and the process of change
- to get to know fellow educators from around the world
- to gain perspective for the new Office of Education
- to inquire together about alternatives to schooling.

More than fifty people were involved in the consultation, and they came from all over the world.

In its preparatory work, the Office of Education at the WCC saw five questions as being fundamental. The Office suggested new answers to these questions:

1. What is education?
   In western culture education had come to be identified with schooling. The time had come for the churches to develop alternatives to schools — to devise ways of educating people apart from sending them to school.

2. What is the purpose of education?
   Traditional education conditions people to accept the structures of their societies. Education must be changed so that it can liberate people and enable them creatively to build a new world.

3. Who decides in education?
   Traditional education is hierarchical and authoritarian. Education, like other institutions in society, must become more democratic.

4. How do we educate?
   Traditional education works on the principle that one person (the teacher) has something (knowledge) which he has to transmit to others who don't have it (pupils). Education must change in such a way that 'educator' and 'educatee' see themselves as 'bound together in a common activity of learning' in order that together they might bring about change in society and in the world.

5. Who gets education?
   Traditional education trains a number of specialized groups of people to run society. This group might be called an 'élite'. Since the pace of change in the world today is so great, many of the skills developed within the élite become obsolete, and we are in danger of being left with

a group of people attempting to impose on a new generation the values, ideas, and structures of an earlier one. In order to prevent this happening, education needs to widen its scope so that more people with a wider range of skills can be encouraged to develop in their own particular directions. Then alternatives will be available when the skills of the élite become obsolete.

Thus the basic thrust of the WCC's Office of Education was worked out: it would help the churches think critically about traditional educational institutions like schools and universities, in the hope that through such critical thinking Christians might use their imaginations to devise alternatives which might be more helpful to the needs of people in the last three decades of the twentieth century.

Many of the questions and problems arising from education which this book attempts to highlight are quite new to a great number of people. Some of them will find the issues difficult to face. They are difficult because they possibly challenge fundamental assumptions which have been accepted uncritically. Each culture transmits some values to its young in a way which leaves it likely that they will accept them uncritically. That is inevitable as well as desirable — it would be an impossible situation if everybody was questioning everything all the time! However, it is clear that there are many things fundamentally wrong with our world, and that some of these wrongs can begin to be put right only if some of the implicit values transmitted through educational systems are examined critically. It is sometimes easier for an outsider to any situation to spot critical questions, than for someone involved on the inside. Also, it is sometimes easier for people in one country to spot some of the problems in their own educational systems when they have begun to be critical of some of the things happening in other parts of the world.

At the same time, it is not sufficient simply to be critical: people need to try out various solutions as well. Although an outsider cannot provide answers, he can make suggestions about things that have been tried in one place, leaving the people in another to decide for themselves whether those solutions can be adapted for their own situations.

There are eight ways in which the Education Office of the WCC tries to help Christians involved in education to achieve these objectives.

1. It has a specialist education staff who travel the world. One of them is Paulo Freire (see page 66). They act as specialist advisers able to help the churches in most countries to think about their educational systems and devise new educational ideas where these are appropriate.

2. It brings people together from different countries and from different regions of the world in conferences and other international gatherings. When people from different cultures meet, all kinds of new ideas emerge.

3. It acts as a postbox for ideas. When any group of Christian education- alists in any part of the world feels it has something to share (a new idea, a new method, a new insight), it can write and tell the staff of the Education Office at the WCC. The staff will then pass it on to others whom they think might be interested.

4. It publishes a newsletter in four languages — English, French, German and Spanish — which is sent free of charge to anyone who wishes to become a subscriber.

5. It gives financial support to individual people who might stand to gain from further education in a foreign country, and to projects which other organizations might not always encourage. For instance, Senegalese village peasants and Portuguese migrant families in a Paris suburb shared in a research project partly supported by the Office.

6. It brings Christian and non-Christian educationalists together in order to encourage them to co-operate with one another. For instance, in September 1973 three hundred delegates attending a UNESCO confer- ence discussed a reference paper prepared by the Office of Education, the YMCA, the YWCA and the World Student Christian Federation. As a result the insights of each side could be of help to the other.

7. It sponsors regular meetings of education officers of regional Christian councils like the All Africa Christian Council, the South-East Asia Christian Council and CELADEC (Latin American Evangelical Commission on Christian Education).

8. It brings educational issues constantly before the churches. At the Fifth Assembly of the WCC held at Nairobi in 1975, there were six conference sections. One of them was devoted to issues raised by 'Education for Liberation and Community'. It was the section of the Assembly which many people found the most difficult. One leading commentator, Bishop Lesslie Newbigin, suggested that one of the reasons for this might be that many Christians involved in education were ahead of the rest of the church in attempting to come to grips with the challenges facing man- kind in the last quarter of the twentieth century.

13. Exploitation — constraint or repression?

## For Discussion

The following is taken from the Report of Section 4 of the Fifth Assembly of the World Council of Churches, December 1975:

> We live in a world of great suffering and disunity; a world shackled to the domination and oppression of human beings by other human beings; a world which persons exploit for their own ends, disrupting the stability of nature; a world in which the major threats to survival now come from human beings themselves given through education the power to be more threatening . . .
>
> Education in too many societies is a consciously used instrument of power; designed to produce those who accept and serve the system; designed to prevent the growth of a critical consciousness which would lead people to want alternatives . . .

The Christian community is placed in the human community to present the total message of Christ and to be a sign of God's liberating power . . .

The hopes and aspirations of much of what the other Sections (of the Fifth Assembly) would wish to see achieved in the Church and in the world will be frustrated or enabled by education. It is time that all of us accepted our responsibility to create and participate in the educative community.

The report went on to make 45 specific recommendations. For further reflection these are worth considering in the light of issues raised in this book. They will be found in *Breaking Barriers: Nairobi 1975*, the official report of the Fifth Assembly of the WCC (edited by David Paton, published by SPCK).

As they prepared for the Fifth Assembly, various working groups of the council studied a document specially prepared for them entitled 'Threats to Survival'. The document argued that mankind lives under the perennial threat of destruction — through population increase beyond that which can be supported by the food, fuel and other raw material resources of the world, through damage to the environment, or through nuclear annihilation. This is the reality which the churches must face if they wish to say and do anything that will be of value to mankind. Those involved in preparing the agenda of the education section for Nairobi suggested that only totally new forms of education could equip the people of this world to perceive and take the necessary action to overcome these threats — traditional forms of education could only provide the framework of mental thought patterns which have produced these problems; and because they have produced the problems, they cannot help humanity to discover solutions without producing new problems. Only an education which undermines the desire for power, wealth, material possessions, competitiveness and individuality can be of real help to mankind in the present age. What is your opinion?

## UNESCO

One of the main functions of UNESCO (the United Nations Educational, Scientific and Cultural Organization) is to help developing countries adapt and modify their educational systems in ways which will be of the greatest help to them. It therefore does most of the things that are also done by the WCC Office of Education, although on a much larger scale. But while UNESCO can be said to be an organization that makes possible an international exchange of ideas on education, its work is not limited to theory and discussion. A great deal of its work involves specific projects in particular countries.

14. The environment.

For instance, it is through UNESCO that the concept of functional literacy has been developed. An experimental programme was set up in twelve countries: Afghanistan, Algeria, Ecuador, Ethiopia, India, Iran, Mali, Niger, Sudan, Syria, Tanzania and Venezuela. The aim was to combine a literacy programme with an economic and social development programme. It is estimated that at least 400,000 adults took part in the programme in 1971.

A major problem concerning education in developing countries has been the training of teachers. It has always been known that the most effective teachers would, in the long term, be those who were indigenous to a country itself. The coming of independence hurried the emigration of European teachers and forced upon many third world countries the need for new teacher-training courses in which a new generation of home-grown educators could be prepared. UNESCO has recently helped establish teacher-training institutes in six African countries (Cameroon, Ethiopia, Ivory Coast, Liberia, Niger, Togo); in these the aim is not simply to train classroom or subject specialists, but to produce rural educators who could adapt their educational methods and objectives to the local community. They thus needed to know as much about rural agriculture and the needs of the village communities as they did about reading and writing and mathematics.

UNESCO has been at the forefront of recommending the widespread use of advanced educational technology. It has encouraged the use of radio and television as educational media. It has recognized that this would involve expensive professional training of specialists able to use the new technology, and has given financial support in order to encourage such training. It has given support to governments in order that they might assess the effectiveness of traditional styles of education, as well as new experiments — it is no good someone in a government office thinking up a bright idea, and then applying it all over the country at great expense, without first having a small, experimental pilot project in a selected area to see if it really works.

UNESCO has always been concerned with educational efficiency: if a particular system works in a particular country, then it needs to be made as widely available as possible at the lowest cost possible. The Ivory Coast, for instance, introduced a scheme for giving ordinary primary education over television. The introduction of the scheme was seen as a means of using experts with particular skills to cover the whole population. But it was immediately recognized that the availability of television in centres of communities where primary children would meet would be uneconomic if the medium was not used for other forms of education as well. So a long-term programme was established under which 16,500 centres would be equipped with television by 1980, and at the same time programmes would be prepared to enable secondary pupils as well as primary to benefit from the medium. Through the introduction of education by television, it is estimated that the increase in available educational facilities will keep pace with the increase in population of school age. This will be achieved at a cost estimated at 44% less than would be the case if the expansion of educational facilities had taken the form of traditional-style schooling.

UNESCO has advocated the notion of lifelong learning, and therefore gives a great deal of encouragement to education directed specifically towards adults, helping them to adapt to life in a fast-changing world.

## For Discussion

In a major report published in 1972 (*Learning to Be*, published by Harraps) an analysis was made of educational development throughout the world, and recommendations submitted to the member states. On the opening pages, the chairman of the group that prepared the report (the International Commission on the Development of Education) set out four assumptions which should dominate educational thinking in the contemporary world; all educational activity needed to take account of these assumptions:

1. We live in a world in which each nation needs to take account of the cultures of others.

2. A concern with democracy implies that each human being has a right to realize his own potential and to share in the building of his own future.

3. 'The aim of development is the complete fulfilment of man, in all the richness of his personality, the complexity of his forms of expression and his various commitments — as individual, member of a family and of a community, citizen and producer, inventor of techniques and creative dreamer.'

4. 'Only an over-all, lifelong education can produce the kind of complete man the need for whom is increasing with the continually more stringent constraints tearing the individual asunder. We should no longer assiduously acquire knowledge once and for all, but learn how to build up a continually evolving body of knowledge all through life — "learn to be".'

## Paulo Freire

In the autumn of 1974, a group of church educationalists from all round the world met for a few days at a conference centre a few miles outside Geneva in Switzerland. Their task was to guide the staff of the WCC Office of Education in putting together part of the programme for the council's forthcoming Fifth Assembly. On the last morning of the conference, Paulo Freire asked the delegates if he might say something to them. He said,

I shall be leaving you all sometime during the morning. I am not asking your permission that I should go — you do not have the right to tell me whether I should stay or whether I might go. You do have the right to know why I intend to go, and I will tell you: today is my son's seventeenth birthday. A few weeks ago I asked him what he would like for his birthday. He told me that he would like the whole family to meet together for a meal in a restaurant in Geneva. So it was arranged, and that is why I shall go: to be with my son on this important day in his life.

This story illustrates a point that is implicit in Paulo Freire's educational philosophy: that people should be free enough to take responsible decisions affecting their own lives. He sees the major function of education as being to make people free to take control of their own lives.

Freire was born in Recife in Brazil in 1921. When he was eight years old, the financial recession which swept across the world left many middle-class families (like that of Paulo Freire) impoverished. It was this experience of poverty which was to have a dominant influence on him in later life. He experienced at first hand the total powerlessness of the poor, and their dependence on those in positions of authority who effectively made all the decisions affecting their lives. He resolved that his life's work should be the liberation of the poor from ignorance, poverty and powerlessness.

After graduating from university he became first a lecturer and then professor of history and of the philosophy of education. As his thinking developed, he was increasingly influenced by Roman Catholic philosophy, by the political thinking of Karl Marx, the existentialist thinking of Jean-Paul Sartre, and the social analysis of psychologists like Erich Fromm.

In 1962 he set up what he called a 'cultural centre' in Recife. This was to be an adult education centre where discussion groups replaced traditional classes. The purpose of these discussion groups was to help 'students' analyse the social and political conditions under which they lived, and to equip them to take appropriate action — to discover what was wrong with society, and to play their part in putting things right.

The work was so effective that a year later he became Secretary of Education and General Co-ordinator of the National Literacy Programme. Thus cultural circles were set up in all the major towns in Brazil, and the 1964 Development Plan set the nation the target of reaching 2 million illiterates in one year.

In Brazil, voting was restricted to those people who could read and write. Therefore political implications followed from Freire's literacy programme: for instance, in the state of Sergipe, which had an electoral role of 9,000 people, 80,000 new voters were added, and in Pernambuco half a million new voters were added to an electoral role of 800,000.

That same year there was a military coup in Brazil, and Freire spent $2\frac{1}{2}$ months in prison because his educational work was regarded as not being in the national interest.

On his release he left the country and went to continue his adult literacy work in Chile — working in the university and for UNESCO. His first book, *Educação como Pratica da Liberdade*, was published in 1967 (the English translation appeared as an essay entitled 'Education as the Practice of Freedom' in *Education for Critical Consciousness*, Sheed and Ward, 1973). In 1969 he went to Harvard University's Centre for the Study of Development and Social Change as a visiting professor, and in 1970 he became a consultant on the staff of the WCC Office of Education.

Paulo Freire's educational method has been briefly described in an earlier section (see page 21). A more detailed account of his method will be found in *Cultural Action for Freedom* (Penguin, 1972), a small and readable book. In this section, attention will be focused on his underlying philosophy.

One of Freire's most important convictions is that no education can ever be neutral — any education will always either domesticate or liberate. On the whole, institutionalized education (schools, colleges, universities) will always tend in the direction of conditioning people towards accepting and working within the basic structures of their society. Generally speaking it is likely that informal education — adult education and literacy courses — will be the most liberating.

He demonstrates this by contrasting his methods with those generally used in schools. He cites the words and stories and sentences used in school books: *Eva saw the grape. The cock crows. The dog barks. Mary likes animals. Charles's father's name is Antonio. Charles is a good, well-behaved and studious boy. Peter did not know how to read. Peter was ashamed. One day, Peter went to school and registered for a night course. Peter's teacher was very good. Peter knows how to read now. Look at Peter's face.* [These lessons are generally illustrated.] *Peter is smiling. He is a happy man. He already has a good job. Everyone ought to follow his example.*

There are two basic things wrong with these sentences and stories: first, they do not arise from the pupils' experience — the teacher or the book prescribes the words which the pupils will learn. Secondly, the teaching transmits the view that society as it exists is basically good — if Peter is suffering unemployment, it is basically his own fault for not having gone to school and become educated.

15. Progress.

The overriding problem with this approach to education is that it treats learners as passive recipients — the learner is like an empty jug into which the teacher pours knowledge. The more knowledge that is poured into a person, the better educated he will be. This is what Freire describes as the 'banking' concept of education — a person accumulates knowledge like money in a bank, and he can draw upon it when necessary. This is a domesticating education.

A liberating education, on the other hand, attempts to encourage pupils to be creative by letting them prescribe, through discussing their own experience, the words which they will learn, and ensures that knowledge will be appropriated (rather than banked) because it will arise from the insights that all the members of the discussion group will together discover in talking about the things that matter most to them.

Freire shows the picture of the slum, and writes the word *favela* (slum) above it. The students and the educator (not 'teacher') talk together about

69

the slum. They describe their living conditions. They try to understand why slums exist. The word *favela* is then split into its three syllables — *fa ve la* — and then each syllable is shown with its family — *fa fe fi fo fu*. The educator then asks the students the difference between the various syllables. Someone will say that they begin with the same letter but end with a different one, which means that they cannot all sound the same. The educator then shows them the different sounds. When all fifteen syllables are shown, the educator asks if it is possible to create something with all these pieces. After a few moments the students begin to form words by combining different syllables — *favela*, *favo*, *fivela*, *luva*, *vale*, *viva*. The students themselves decide which words they will learn, and many will arise from their earlier discussion.

Freire argues that education either enables people to be critically aware of social and political conditions, or it tries to avoid real-life questions and thus attempts to fit people into the existing order.

Freire regards all human beings as creators. He also sees man as incomplete — as on a journey through life in which he is continually learning and giving of himself to his brothers and sisters in the human family. He believes that all human beings are in some measure oppressed (even those whom some regard as oppressors). He maintains that human beings can journey together through life, being open to and learning from one another. All human beings, oppressors and oppressed alike, because they are in some ways all oppressed can together break down the domesticating oppressions which make them less than human by together discovering a liberation which will enable them to create new and more just social and political conditions.

Paulo Freire is now known all over the world. While clearly it is sometimes inappropriate to transplant his methods, the ideas which underlie them seem to be valid in all situations. His conviction that people should become aware of the way in which educational systems condition them to accept, rather than to try to bring about change in the world is as valid in England, Sweden, the United States, the Middle East, Russia, Africa and India as it was and is in Latin America.

# POSTSCRIPT

For many people, to talk about education is to talk about schools. This book has attempted to show that education and schooling are not the same thing. In fact there could be circumstances in which schooling could be quite uneducational. Education is about helping people to learn in order that they might give of themselves to their fellow human beings. The word *education* comes from the Latin word *educare*, which means 'to lead out'. Because, within the Christian view of things at least, each human being is unique and has a priceless contribution of his own to make to mankind, the 'leading out' with which education is concerned should aim to affirm that uniqueness within the community of mankind. It should strive to enable people and communities to grow in directions appropriate to themselves, rather than *prescribe* the ways in which they should develop.

When we begin to talk about education in these terms, we cannot avoid also talking about an enormous range of other issues as well – politics, economics, power, human exploitation of man and his environment, community, government, international development. Life has become more complex than mankind has ever known it before. All the perplexing issues of life are interrelated.

The World Council of Christian Education, meeting in Lima, Peru, in 1971, for the last time before it became a part of the WCC, sent its message to the churches in these words: 'To educate is not so much to teach as it is to become committed to a reality in and with people; it is to learn to live, to encourage creativity in ourselves and others; and under God and his power, to liberate mankind from the bonds that prevent the development of God's image.'